Copyright © 2024 Anna Donahue.

All rights reserved. No part of this book may be used or reproduced by any means, graphic, electronic, or mechanical, including photocopying, recording, taping or by any information storage retrieval system without the written permission of the author except in the case of brief quotations embodied in critical articles and reviews.

WestBow Press books may be ordered through booksellers or by contacting:

WestBow Press
A Division of Thomas Nelson & Zondervan
1663 Liberty Drive
Bloomington, IN 47403
www.westbowpress.com
844-714-3454

Because of the dynamic nature of the Internet, any web addresses or links contained in this book may have changed since publication and may no longer be valid. The views expressed in this work are solely those of the author and do not necessarily reflect the views of the publisher, and the publisher hereby disclaims any responsibility for them.

New King James Version Scriptures marked NKJV are taken from the NEW KING JAMES VERSION (NKJV): Scripture taken from the NEW KING JAMES VERSION®. Copyright© 1982 by Thomas Nelson, Inc. Used by permission. All rights reserved.

Interior Image Credit: Beatriz McDonald

ISBN: 979-8-3850-3752-0 (sc)
ISBN: 979-8-3850-3888-6 (hc)
ISBN: 979-8-3850-3751-3 (e)

Library of Congress Control Number: 2024923109

Print information available on the last page.

WestBow Press rev. date: 12/02/2024

This book is dedicated to
Ellie Jane Donahue
our 2nd grandchild; a granddaughter!
Ellie, your name means 'God is my light' and you have already lived up to your name as
you bring so much light, joy and
love wherever you go!
May you continue to shine His light all the days of your life!

Contents

Abraham: A Lesson in Obedience 5

David: A Lesson in Boldness 11

Gideon: A Lesson in Courage 17

Queen Esther: A Lesson in Bravery 25

The Woman at the Well: A Lesson in Hope 29

DO YOU SEE WHAT I SEE?

What God Sees When He Looks at You!

By Anna Donahue

As our story opens we find three small children leaving their schoolhouse and walking towards home. As they continue their journey, they come across a small pond. The three of them lean over and peer into the cool waters of the pond. They see their reflections.

They talk about what their teacher taught them that day. She taught that the people in the Bible who did great things for God, weren't always the bravest, or the smartest or the strongest!

In fact, just the opposite was true. The people in the Bible were often weak, scared, and very shy until God got ahold of them! Once they met God, He showed them who He made them to be and they were changed!

As the children peer over their reflections, they, too, wonder, "who has God made ME to be?"

ABRAHAM
a lesson in obedience

Abraham was a man of great faith.
And it was through Abraham's family line that the Savior of the world came.

But it wasn't always an easy journey.
It required big faith, courage and obedience on Abraham's part.

Before knowing God, Abraham was a moon worshipper.
But he met God who called Abraham on the journey of a lifetime.

God asked Abraham to leave everything that he knew, behind.
God helped Abraham find a land that God had marked out for him.
This land would be for Abraham and for his children's children.
Here, Abraham and his people became God's people.

"So Abram left Haran as the Lord had told him."
-Genesis 12:4

"He responded obediently because he knew that he had heard from God."
-Acts 7:2

That act of obedience changed history! As Abraham and his family continued towards their new land, God spoke to Abraham. He made a promise to him stating that in this new land, Abraham would become a father of many nations and that he would have as many children as the number of stars in the sky.

"Then He brought him outside and said, "Look now toward heaven, and count the stars if you are able to number them." And He said to him, "So shall your descendants be."
-Genesis 15:5

"As for Me, behold, my covenant is with thee, and thou shalt be a father of many nations."
-Genesis 17:4

Can you imagine? Abraham gazed at the night sky in awe!
"What is happening?" he must have thought!

God said to Abraham, "Abraham, Do You See What I see?
You are not just a moon worshipper! I have so much more
for you! I see you as a father of many nations!"

And it doesn't end with Abraham! God is calling all of us to follow Him into new
territory every day. He sees you and all that you can become in Him!

Abraham's life helps us to understand this. It can be scary at times leaving
all that is safe and going somewhere that you don't know. But when it is
God doing the leading, you can be sure that His plan is the best plan and
that He will see you through to safety every step of the way!

"Lord, help me to obey!"

DAVID
a lesson in BOLDNESS

When we think of David, our first thoughts go towards the huge battle that he fought and won against Goliath, the large enemy of Israel. And that IS a great way to think of David. But there are other areas in which he is well known.

David was a great musician, "the sweet psalmist of Israel" (2 Samuel 23:1). As a young boy, he practiced the harp on the sheep fields of Bethlehem. As he grew, he wrote songs or Psalms, as the Bible calls them, that fill nearly half of the Book of Psalms in the Bible.

2. David was also a warrior. His courage to stand up to
and defeat Goliath is known all over the world.

3. And finally, David was a king; one of the best kings of all time.
How did David get such confidence, such strength?

How did he go from watching sheep to being one of the greatest kings in all of Israel?
David loved God. He looked to Him for everything. As he grew in
his love for God, his faith and trust in God grew also.
The Bible says that David was a man after God's own heart.

"The Lord has sought for Himself a man after His own heart,..."
-1 Samuel 13:14

That means that he loved God so much and wanted to please
Him all of the days of his life!

God was saying to David, "David, Do You See What I See?
You are not simply a young shepherd boy, but I see you as one of the greatest
musicians of all time! I see you as a mighty warrior! I see you as a king!"
What a powerful lesson for us to learn as well. When facing the giants in our lives,
like David, if we will look to God, and love Him with all of our heart, He will
help us be strong and beat those giants down to the ground.
He will then show us all of the amazing plans that He has for our lives.

"Lord, help me to be bold!"

GIDEON
a lesson in courage

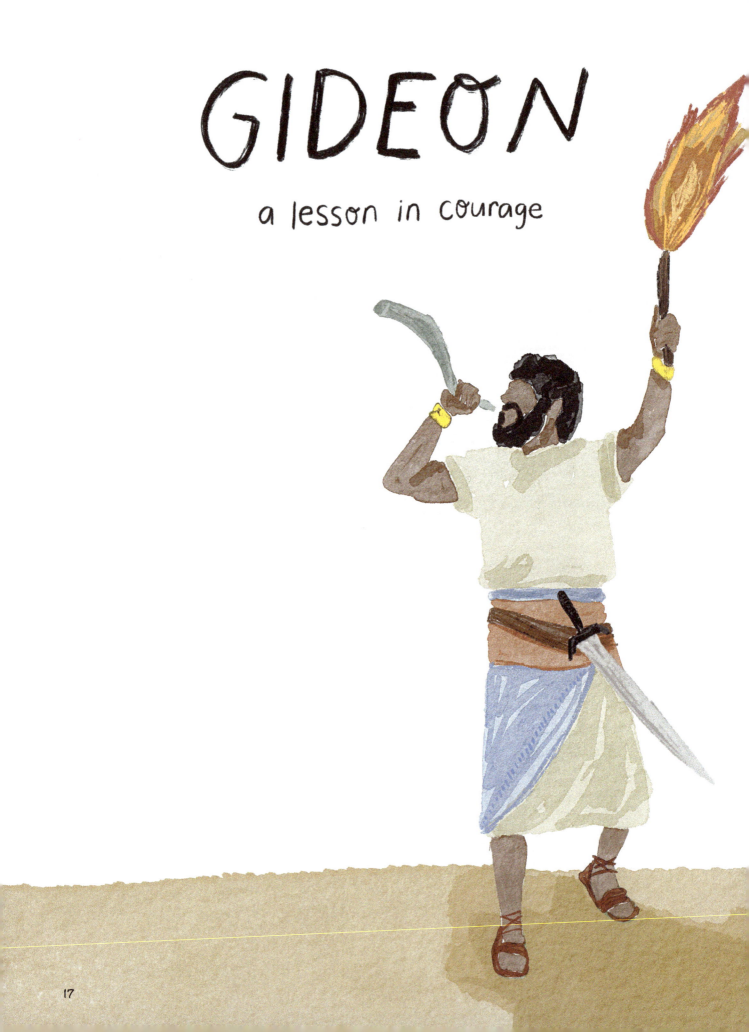

Gideon was one of the most unlikely heroes in the entire Old Testament.
In fact, if ever there was someone with whom you would think would never be used greatly by God, it would have been Gideon.

At the time we met Gideon, war was breaking out against Israel, Gideon's people.
But where was Gideon? He was hiding! He was very much afraid.

But an Angel of the Lord appeared to him and called him a mighty man of valor.
The Angel then told Gideon that he would be the one to free his people from the enemy.

"And the Angel of the Lord appeared to him, and said to him,
"The Lord is with you, you mighty man of valor!"
-Judges 6:12

"What? How can this be?" Gideon thought.
"How can I be the one God is choosing to save our people from the enemy?"

He was hiding from the enemy. He felt weak and small and not enough.

But God saw Gideon differently! He said to Gideon,

"Gideon, Do You See What I See? You are not just a frightened man hiding! I see you as a mighty man of valor! I see you as bold and courageous!"

And just as the Angel of the Lord said, with God's help, Gideon led the children of Israel to a great victory!

Like Gideon, maybe you too struggle with being afraid. Maybe you are shy! Maybe you think, "I am scared, I'm not brave like other kids."

But none of that is true. God loves and wants YOU!

Throw out the fear and look to God instead. Like Gideon, you will become strong and do great things for Him!

"Lord, help me to have courage!"

QUEEN ESTHER
a lesson in bravery

The story of Queen Esther is one of the most inspiring stories of the Bible. Queen Esther allowed God to guide her. And Queen Esther did a mighty work for Him. Because she obeyed God, she saved thousands of people from death.

Did she start out that way? Was she of high birth or top rank or listed as one of society's status symbols?

Not at all! In fact, Esther was an orphan. She was a young orphaned Jewish girl who had been shipped off to a foreign land. Yet none of that kept God from exalting her to the position where He wanted her to be.

Through a series of events, Esther won a beauty contest. She was placed in a palace in Persia to live with the king of Persia as his wife.

But at the palace, she got word from her cousin Mordecai that an evil man named Haman wanted to destroy all of the Jews in the area.

Unfortunately, Esther was a Jew, and her life was in danger. Little did Haman know that that means Esther herself would also be destroyed because she too was a Jew!

Mordecai told Esther to rise up and stop this.
He wanted Esther to go to the king and plead for the Jews' lives.
But Esther knew that anyone who went to the king
uninvited would have their head chopped off.
What to do? Esther was scared.
But Mordecai encouraged Esther to consider that she might have a greater calling.
After fasting and praying Esther realized that she must
go to the king and tell him what the evil man Haman was doing.
She risked her life but she went forward anyway and trusted God every step of the way.

We can hear God saying, "Esther! Do You See What I See?
You are not just a shy orphan girl living in a foreign land with no hope!
You are a mighty woman of God, called for such a time as this! I have chosen
you to save your nation." And with God's help, that is exactly what she did!
How about you? Have you ever faced a scary situation and had to
find the bravery to go forward, trusting in God? You can do it!
God is in you! He will help you!

"Yet who knows whether you have come to the kingdom for such a time as this?"
-Esther 4:14

"Lord, help me to be brave!"

THE WOMAN AT THE WELL
a lesson in hope

Our story opens with a woman from an area called Samaria, coming to get water from a very famous well known as 'Jacob's Well'.

Most women of the village came to the well in the morning to avoid the hot sun. But this woman came at the hottest time of day. She came because she knew no one else from the village would be there. Sadly, the people in her village treated her badly.

But Jesus sees in people what they can become! And He saw this woman differently!

Tired from His journey, He came to the well to get a drink of water. He asked the woman for a drink. She was surprised because He was kind and spoke to her!

God knew that this woman, if given the chance, would turn from the way she was then living to living a much better life. She just needed the love of our heavenly Father to do so. As their conversation continued, Jesus shared with this woman that He had Living Water to give to her. And with this water, she would never be thirsty again.

"How could that be?" she thought. "How could you have such water?" But Jesus wasn't talking about being thirsty for water that comes from a well. He was talking about being thirsty for water that comes from God. This water, (water that comes from God), is 'Living Water' and that once we drink of it (Him) we never thirst again!

"Jesus answered and said to her, "Whoever drinks of this water will thirst again but whoever drinks of the water that I shall give him will never thirst. But the water that I shall give him will become in him a fountain of water springing up into everlasting life."

-John 4:13-14

"He who believes in Me, as the Scripture has said,
out of his heart will flow rivers of living water."

-John 7:38

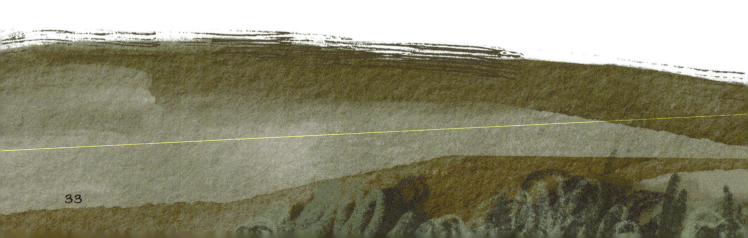

The woman realized that this was Jesus the Christ Who was talking to her. She was filled with joy! She dropped her water pot, and ran to tell others!

So in spite of what people thought about or said about this woman, Jesus saw through it all. He chose her to be the one to show Who He truly was: Jesus the Christ; the One Who came to earth to set men free!

We can hear Him saying to this woman, "Woman of Samaria, Do You See What I See?

I don't see you as a woman with all of your past sins and bad mistakes. Rather, I see you as a daughter of the Lord; a woman who has a heart to worship God and who will spread the Good News to others!"

Like the woman at the well, maybe you, too, have had others treat you unkindly. Maybe you have done some bad things and you are very sorry. God sees you! He loves you! And He says to YOU today, "I forgive you! I love you! Go and do all that I have put in your heart to do! You are a Good News carrier for Me!"

"Lord, help me to have hope!"

The entire Bible is filled with people who started out one
way and then God grabbed ahold of them and said, "Hey! I see you!
I have a plan for you. And it is good!
It will go above and beyond ANYTHING you can ask, imagine or think."

There's Sarah, Abraham's wife. In her early years she could
not have children. But God saw things differently. God
saw Sarah as not only the mother of one child, but many.
He called her the mother of nations. (Genesis 17:15-16)

Or what about Paul?
Earlier called Saul, God saw
him, saved him and equipped him
to bring the teachings of
Jesus to the Gentiles!
God chose him to become
one of the greatest
missionaries of all time! (Acts 9:1-31)

And then there was Noah. When all the crowd was going the wrong way, Noah chose not to. The people in Noah's day were doing very bad things. In fact, it got so bad that God wanted to wipe everything out and start over with just one family: Noah's family. God told Noah to build a large boat.

"I am about to destroy the earth with a flood. But I will save you and your household and two of every animal. I will start over."
-Genesis 6:1

Noah was teased by his family and everyone else on the earth at that time. They made fun of him for building the boat! But God said to Noah, "Noah! Do You See What I See? Where others are doing wrong in my sight, you are not! I will destroy the earth but I will save you and your family and start over!" And God did just that.

And what about Joshua and Caleb? When others went to see what the Promised Land looked like before they were to go and live there, most came back and said that they could not make it in the land. They even called themselves grasshoppers! But when Joshua and Caleb went and looked at the land, they saw things differently. They saw themselves as strong and able! (Numbers 13-14)

And then of course, Mary-the mother of Jesus. She went from being a simple young girl to becoming the mother of Jesus. We can hear the Lord saying to Mary,

"Mary, Do You See What I See? You are not just a simple young girl of a small village, but Mary, I see you as the mother of Jesus!" (Luke 1:26-38)

And what about Jesus Himself? Man could not `see` that Jesus was the Savior of the world sent from heaven to save people from their sins! But that is exactly what He did! (Matthew 1:21)

Others may not see you, or if they do, they may see you incorrectly. But God sees you! And He knows what He sees when He looks at you!

"It's in Christ that we find out who we are and what we are living for. Long before we first heard of Christ and got our hopes up, He had His eye on us, had designs on us for glorious living, part of the overall purpose He is working out in everything and everyone."
-Ephesians 1:11-12 MSG.

How about you?
Maybe you look at yourself and wonder,
"How God? How can I 'see' my life the way you do?"

I have written this short acronym that might help you.
And remember: God wants us to 'see'! He is not hiding His will from us.

S-I-G-H-T

S -Start with God

Always go back to the beginning. Start with God. That may sound easy but oftentimes you will find yourself wanting to start with yourself. When we start with ourselves, we might think, "What am I good at?" But to start with God, we can think, "What does God ask of me?" or "What gifts has He given me?"

God is the One Who designed you. He is the One Who knows all of the gifts and talents that are placed inside of you! He is the One Who will have your answers. Go to Him in prayer and talk to Him about your life.

"Message-Everything got started in Him and finds its purpose in Him."
-Col.1:16

S -Can also stand for Spirit. God's plan will come out of your spirit. It's an inside job.

God's Spirit helps us to make our way through life. He shows us what to do.

"...Eye has not seen, nor ear heard, neither have entered into the heart of man, the things which God has prepared for them that love Him..."but God hath revealed them unto us by His Spirit." The Spirit searcheth all things, yea, the deep things of God."
-1 Cor. 2:9-10

I -Invest in the Word of God! "Invest means to spend time or effort on something in order to reach a big goal." When you invest in the Word of God, you spend time learning God's truths. You work hard to learn what He says. You then obey what He says and that's when change takes place!

"But He answered and said, "It is written, 'Man shall not live by bread alone, but by every word that proceeds from the mouth of God.'"
-Matthew. 4:4

G -Grow!-Bloom right where you are!

As you pray, you are getting pictures of what God has created you to do and to be!

But chances are those pictures are still very small. You need to grow!

Spend time with God every day!

Before you know it, you will begin to 'see' what you once only dreamed of!

H -Holy Spirit

We never do this alone! God has given us His wonderful Holy Spirit to help us!

| T | -Trust/Faith is being developed.

"All things are working together for the good to those who love the Lord and are the called according to His purpose."
-Romans 8:28

God's plans for you are amazing. They are above anything you would have ever thought.

Let's pray together:
"Dear Lord, I have so many fun ideas and thoughts running through my mind of what I would like to do and be! But I want to talk with you about them first. I want to do what you want me to do. Help me to see myself the way You see me! With your help, I can do anything that you put in my heart to do. Thank you Lord. I love you! In Jesus' Name! Amen!"

Anna Donahue is a vibrant Bible Teacher, Author and Speaker, whose passion is to teach, encourage and equip people everywhere to know Christ, walk in their divine destinies, and live the overcoming life found in Christ alone. In addition to writing, 'Do You See What I See?' Anna has written another fully illustrated faith based children's book, entitled 'Did You Know?' She has written two other books, 'Power, Love and a Sound Mind', and 'Uprooting Rejection' and she has written three mini books, 'Determined', 'It's Time for a Fresh Start', and 'Identity'.

You can reach Anna through her website:
www.annadonahueministries.com

Beatriz McDonald is a gifted Artist, Illustrator, and Photographer. She has illustrated her own children's book entitled 'Big Easy Counting' which is reaching the greater New Orleans, Louisiana area. In addition to illustrating 'Do You See What I See?' Beatriz has also illustrated a fully faith based childrens book entitled 'Did You Know?'. She has also illustrated 'The Pink Starfish', a book that encourages children to celebrate what makes them unique. Beatriz's passion is to inspire and encourage people of all ages to use their creative gifts and talents to advance the Kingdom of Heaven. Beatriz is a devoted wife, daughter, sister and friend.

You can reach Beatriz through her website:
www.beatrizmcdonald.com